The Quantum Leap Strategy for Personal Development

The Quantum Leap Strategy for Personal Development

Table Of Contents

Foreword

Personal development or the actions necessary to improve one' mental and physical self or one's performance can exist on different levels; on an individual level, developing other people and beyond that it is a field of practice and research. We have all the info to get you started here.

Personal Development Quantum Leap Strategy

Grow leaps and bounds and stay there!

Chapter 1:

Personal Development Basics

Synopsis

Personal development can be undertaken in a variety of ways and making use of a range of tools and teaching techniques. It is possible for a person to work on their own personal development independently of others by using self help books, videos and a range of other materials available. Other individuals could choose to make use of professional personal developers such as counselors or life coaches.

The Basics

At the individual level it includes improving self awareness and self knowledge. Attention is given the ways that can be found to improve wealth and health and lifestyle.

An individual's personal skills are worked upon to improve the person's social ability. Improvements in this area as well as the person's enriching performance in social situations can also improve the individual's employability. Some individuals choose to focus their spirituality to improve their quality of life.

Beyond self help personal development includes developing other people. This form of personal development may take place through the role of teachers. Education systems are designed to enhance personal development and self growth.

The academic teaching given in institutions runs parallel with the assistance given by teachers to enhance the personal development of their charges.

Mentors offer enormous scope in the area of personal development and can be paid individuals or working in the voluntary capacity such as a fellow colleague or relative. Some people choose specifically to employ a life coach to help them plan out their personal development program and to guide them through it.

Professional development is also a field of practice and research. The methods employed include learning, programs, assessment systems, tools and techniques.

Like any form of development, personal development makes use of frameworks or criteria to assess whether change has occurred. The frameworks include goals, strategies, levels and feedback systems.

Chapter 2:

Synopsis

Any individuals giving careful consideration to embarking on a self development program of any kind need first to have a critical look at themselves. It is essential to know oneself well in order to ascertain what area or areas need improvement. It is all too easy to feel that life isn't going well and feel that things need to be improved but unless it is known exactly where there are areas of weakness it is difficult for things to be improved.

Changing

Whilst it might be a slow and sometimes painful and exhausting exercise it is necessary to examine many facets of one's life. Consideration will need to be given to all or some of the following; personal happiness, one's health and state of physical and mental wellbeing, personal wealth, work performance and career path, relationships one has with others and personal aspirations.

A person's physical and mental good health is fundamental to their performance in all aspects of life. It will be necessary to analyze one's physical health to decide whether there are areas that need focus to heal and be improved upon.

This may be something simple like taking a hearing or vision test. Diet and cardio vascular fitness are other areas that need to be considered.

A good look at one's own mental health might be able to determine if an individual is affected by stress or anxiety and determine whether or not they are areas of life that need to be worked on.

We are all engaged in relationships of some kind or other. Giving time to reflect on those that we have will allow us to ascertain whether they are positive or not. Consideration would then need to be given to whether relationships need to be terminated, developed or improved.

Most individuals, unless retired, have to spend a considerable proportion of their life in employment. Time analyzing job performance and satisfaction is crucial to self reflection. Closely linked with career and work is personal wealth and this is another area that needs very careful consideration.

Chapter 3:

Synopsis

Once a person has decided that they want to commence upon a personal development program they should then undertake some critical self analysis.

It is only by first having a critical look at their own selves that individuals can work out what areas of their lives need attention. This process of self examination can be very painful but it is essential that it is undertaken.

Decide

After having a critical look at themselves it might be that there are several components of their life and being that require to be worked upon.

Many individuals can be very hard on themselves and simply believe that everything is wrong with themselves and they need to work on every component. Such way of thinking is likely to bring about failure. It is essential to be more specific.

After having looked at themselves in a critical way and noting down the areas for self development individuals should then rank the areas according to how important they believe the areas are to improved personal performance.

Such rankings will differ from individual to individual. What is important is that the individual realizes which area is to be focused upon first.

By placing attention on one or very limited number of areas to begin with it is more likely that success will be achieved rather than striving to make many changes or learn too many strategies at once.

When the area for personal development has been determined the individual must then decide exactly what the outcome should be. It is unworkable to have undefined or woolly goals such as "I want to be happier." Precision is what is needed here so that there is a clear objective to work towards. Once that objective is clearly defined then the task involved to bring about its outcome can be broken down into achievable steps.

Chapter 4:

Write Out A Personal Development Plan

Synopsis

Once an individual has determined that they want to improve their life by undertaking a form of personal development, in order to succeed, they then need to formulate a personal development plan.

A personal development plan is all about the individual and what the individual wants to accomplish. Personal development plans are devised in many ways and there are no hard and fast rules.

Have A Plan

Before commencing it is essential that the person knows exactly what they are trying to accomplish. They should write down what they want and how they intend to achieve it.

It can be useful for a person to consider their life purpose and define what they were born to do, to note their dreams and also their short, medium and long term goals.

Thought should also be given to the person's own values and beliefs and what they want to be noted for and envisage their ideal self. It would be useful to note down mistakes that have been made previously and the lessons that have been learned from them.

A very simple template to use when drafting a personal development plan would consist of a page for each development area divided into four columns titled over 1 year. Over 3 years, over 5 years and over 10 years.

Development area page titles could be career, personal, finances, physical body and social. But as was stated earlier there are no rules and personal development plans are just that; personal.

Once the pages have been titled write in each column what you want to accomplish and why. Then write how you can achieve this. Specifically note what actions you are going to take.

There are tools that could be used and should be considered to ensure success. Seek out events, courses, classes, books and seminars that could support the person achieving their objective.

Note any supporters and mentors who could be worked with. There is support available and the individual should bear in mind that it is a personal development plan and it will take time to achieve objectives.

Chapter 5:

Learn How To Use Imagery To Manifest

Synopsis

Imagery is an ancient technique that has its roots in the Hindu Monistic theory of the universe. The advocates of imagery believe they have the ability to affect the outer world by changing one's own thoughts.

Imagine

Famously the American Wallace Wattles in his book "Science of Getting Rich" proclaimed creative visualization as the main technique for realizing one's goals. Imagery as a technique to manifest, wealth and positive outcomes in life is practiced throughout the world and has many advocates.

Imagery is another term for creative visualization and is the technique which underlies the power of positive thinking that is much used by athletes and sports persons to enhance performance. Practitioners believe in creating a detailed picture or plan of what one wants to happen and to visualize it over and over again with all the senses.

As the imagery is being imagined the practitioners give thought to what they see, what they feel, hear and can smell.

Whilst there are skeptics out there are many individuals you practice the technique and believe it to be a science claiming that its effects are measurable.

Any individuals embarking on a personal development program would be well advised to include imagery as part of the program. Time needs to be set aside each day to undertake imagery.

A quiet area needs to found and the mind needs to be cleared of thought. It is important to bring about a feeling of calm and tranquility and peace.

Regular deep breathing whilst clearing the mind will help. The event or outcome that is to be manifested is then envisaged repeatedly. An individual working towards a promotion could image the event repeatedly or an overweight individual could image themselves slim.

The belief is that the energy within the world will bring these events into being. Imagery is a powerful tool and should be utilized in personal development.

Chapter 6:

Synopsis

Believing in yourself, or self confidence, is the sureness of feeling that you are equal to the task on hand. Confidence is contagious and self confident people carry with them an aura of success and inspire confidence of a successful outcome in other people. Self confident people appear positive and in control.

This Is Crucial

Self confidence is a very important attribute to have or to cultivate if it is lacking. Developing self confidence should be part of every personal development program of anyone with low self esteem.

Past performance accomplishments are strong contributors to confidence.

When an individual performs successfully they generate confidence and will indicate that they are willing to attempt something more difficult. In a situation where personal confidence is low it is critical to recall times and events that have been successful and to use imagery to generate confidence once more.

Self confidence can be increased by being around self confident and successful people by adapting an "if they can do then so can I" approach to the situation. Reasoning in this way will improve personal performance.

Important occasions can create self doubt even in the most confident of individuals. When nervous or anxious it is more important than ever to regain control and appear confident. Imaging is a very important tool to use to boost self confidence in this situation. Deep breathing and visualizing the successful outcome repeatedly will greatly help.

Wrapping Up

Whilst confidence is contagious so is lack of confidence. It is essential for all individuals that they project a positive and confident image in order to be taken seriously. Performance and success can change simply as a result of the image being perceived by an audience. As individuals we are all responsible for our image and aura or confidence and we must remember that when lady luck is not shining it is us who are responsible for determining how confident we feel.

www.ingramcontent.com/pod-product-compliance
Lightning Source LLC
LaVergne TN
LVHW050313200726

843509LV00015B/3303